HIRAGANA
From Zero!

George Trombley
Yukari Takenaka

Visit our website to meet other students in the chat room or forums.
JapaneseFromZero.com

Distributed worldwide by:
From Zero, LLC
10624 S. Eastern Ave. #A769,
Henderson, NV 89052.

First edition, 2011
Second edition, Nov, 2014 (major update)

Questions, Comments, Wholesale?
book@learnfromzero.com

Hiragana From Zero!

About this book

Introduction

☐ Welcome to HIRAGANA FROM ZERO!

Learning to write hiragana can be intimidating at first, but don't worry! Our method is designed to lead you step-by-step through the basics of hiragana.

☐ Japanese characters

WHAT ARE THESE STRANGE LETTERS? The Japanese language uses a set of symbols called *hiragana* (to spell Japanese words), *katakana* (to spell foreign words), and *kanji* (to represent entire words or names). This book will teach you hiragana followed by katakana character by characer to gradually build up your understanding and familiarity.

Until you can read hiragana, this book will use *ro–maji* (Japanese words spelled with Roman letters), but as each lesson progresses, we will continually substitute them with the hiragana you've learned. By the end of this book, you will be able to read and write hiragana and katakana!

☐ Japanese punctuation facts

HERE ARE SOME QUICK FACTS about Japanese writing to help you get started.

UPPERCASE/LOWERCASE
There are no upper and lower cases in Japanese. In English, we learn to write both *A* and *a*, but in Japanese, あ is always あ.

PERIODS
Japanese periods are small circles instead of dots.
Kore wa hon desu. → in hiragana becomes → これは ほんです。

How this book works

This book uses *Japanese From Zero's* PROGRESSIVE SYSTEM of teaching. As you learn new hiragana, we will immediately replace the roman letters (ro–maji) with the hiragana you have just learned. For example, after you learn あ (which sounds like "ah") we will mix it into the example words.

English	Before	After	After book
you	anata	あ nata	あなた
dog	inu	い nu	いぬ
house	ie	いえ	いえ
mother	okaasan	お ka あ san	おかあさん

About the authors

Author George Trombley is a professional Japanese interpreter who over the past 16 years has interpreted at corporations such as Microsoft, Motorola, NTT DoCoMo, Varian Medical, and in countries throughout North America, Europe, Asia and the Middle East.

George Trombley and his wife Yukari Takenaka formed a Japanese Language School in 1998 and since then, the live classroom courses have formed the basis for the *Japanese From Zero!* textbook series and the YesJapan.com interactive language learning website.

Write in this book!

From Zero! is designed to be an <u>interactive workbook</u> where you can take personal notes, add new words or phrases of your own, and develop your writing from hopeless/crazy/illegible to expert-level.

Every time you write in this book, you're making your connection to Japanese a little bit stronger - we guarantee it!

Ganbatte kudasai!
George Trombley
Yukari Takenaka

Pronunciation Guide & The Basics

Why Learn Hiragana and Katakana?

All of your life you have been reading the alphabet a certain way. You have learned that the letter combination "TO" sounds like the number 2. This instinct may be hard to overcome at first.

In Japanese, "TO" is read as "TOW". If you read this like you were taught in grade school your Japanese accent would be pretty bad! Learning the hiragana and katakana solves this problem.

Before you can learn hiragana and katakana, you will need to know how Japanese is represented in the Roman alphabet. This lesson will teach you how Japanese is pronounced. Let's get started!

The Japanese Writing Systems

There are three Japanese writing systems:
- hiragana (pronounced "hear-uh-gah-nah")
- katakana (pronounced "kah-tah-kah-nah")
- kanji (pronounced "kahn-jee")

Kanji are Chinese characters, and each one has a specific meaning. Many kanji have multiple meanings and can be read different ways. Hiragana and katakana are phonetic characters derived from the more complicated kanji. They each represent a sound and do not have meaning by themselves.

The three writing systems are used together to write Japanese. Hiragana and kanji are used together to form all Japanese words. Katakana is mostly used to represent words of foreign origin or any word that was not originally Japanese. In daily life the combination of these three systems, plus roman letters called "ro–maji", are used in all types of media.

Japanese Pronunciation

Anyone can sound great in Japanese. Although English is made up of over a thousand possible sounds, Japanese has many less. A little over a hundred sounds are all you need to speak Japanese.

For this reason, it is much easier for English-speaking people to learn natural Japanese pronunciation than it is for Japanese speakers to learn natural English pronunciation. With just a few exceptions, Japanese sounds are based on the following five vowel sounds:

❑ Normal vowels

These sounds are short and simple, with no glide or lengthening.

Roman Letter	Sounds Like	Example
a	**ah** as in **father**	akai (red)
i	**ee** as in **see**	inochi (life)
u	**oo** as in **zoo**	uma (horse)
e	**eh** as in **men**	ebi (shrimp)
o	**oh** as in **boat**	otoko (man)

Now let's look at some more sounds. Use the same pronunciation as above for the sound sets listed below.

ka, ki, ku, ke, ko	sa, shi, su, se, so	pa, pi, pu, pe, po
ga, gi, gu, ge, go	na, ni, nu, ne, no	ba, bi, bu, be, bo

The following phonetic sounds are based on the "normal vowel" sounds listed above. The only difference is how the sound starts.

Roman Letter	Sounds Like	Example
ka	kah	**ka** (mosquito)
shi	shee	**shi**ru (to know)
tsu	tsoo	**tsu**ru (crane bird)
ne	neh	**ne**ko (cat)
po	poh	tan**po**po (dandelion)

❑ Double vowels

To display a lengthened vowel, this book will use A, I, U, E, or O after the vowel sound that is to be lengthened. This style mimics how lengthening is done when writing in hiragana and katakana.

Roman Letters	Sound	Example
aa, a–	**ah** as in f**a**ther	ok**aa**san (mother)
ii, i–	**ee** as in s**ee**	oj**ii**san (grandfather)
uu, u–	**oo** as in z**oo**	zu**tsuu** (headache)
ei, ee, e–	**eh** as in m**en**	on**ee**san (older sister)
ou, oo, o–	**oh** as in b**oat**	**mou**fu (blanket)

Words that are written in katakana often use a "–" as the "lengthener" instead of a repeating vowel (shown above). You'll learn more about katakana after the hiragana section.

Example Words (with double vowels)

kyoutsuu	common	otousan	father
satou	sugar	obaasan	grandmother
heiwa	peace	sensou	war
yasashii	kind	isogashii	busy

❑ Long versus short sounds

The meaning of a Japanese word can be changed by lengthening just one syllable.

Examples

ie	house
iie	no
obasan	aunt
obaasan	grandmother
ojisan	uncle
ojiisan	grandfather

❏ Double consonants

Some Japanese words use double consonant sounds. Double consonants such as 'kk', 'pp', 'tt', and 'cch' must be stressed more than a single consonant to show the correct meaning of a word.

Examples

roku	number six
ro<u>kk</u>u	rock (music)
uta	a song
u<u>tt</u>a	sold (past tense verb)
mata	again
ma<u>tt</u>a	waited (past tense verb)

Lesson 1: Hiragana あいうえお

Some History れきし

Hiragana was created by a Buddhist monk over 1200 years ago (AD 774-835). At that time women were not allowed to learn the very intricate kanji. After hiragana was introduced, women were able to express themselves in the written form. It is due to hiragana that women authored many of the first published works in Japan.

Hiragana character samples

あかさたなはまやらわん

Katakana was created by using portions of kanji, while the more rounded hiragana was created by simplifying kanji. Children learn hiragana first, then katakana, and finally kanji.

Katakana character samples

アカサタナハマヤラワン

In 2010 the Japanese Ministry of Education added to the original 1,945 commonly used kanji, called the *Joyou Kanji,* upping the total required kanji to 2,136. By the 6th grade, the average Japanese student knows half of the *Joyou Kanji.*

Kanji character samples

安加左太奈波末也良和毛

The goal ゴール

When you complete the hiragana section you will be able to read and write the hiragana symbols shown below + the combined hiragana.

46 standard hiragana

あ a	か ka	さ sa	た ta	な na	は ha	ま ma	や ya	ら ra	わ wa
い i	き ki	し shi	ち chi	に ni	ひ hi	み mi		り ri	
う u	く ku	す su	つ tsu	ぬ nu	ふ fu	む mu	ゆ yu	る ru	を wo
え e	け ke	せ se	て te	ね ne	へ he	め me		れ re	
お o	こ ko	そ so	と to	の no	ほ ho	も mo	よ yo	ろ ro	ん n

25 altered hiragana

が ga	ざ za	だ da		ば ba	ぱ pa		
ぎ gi	じ ji	ぢ ji		び bi	ぴ pi		
ぐ gu	ず zu	づ zu		ぶ bu	ぷ pu		
げ ge	ぜ ze	で de		べ be	ぺ pe		
ご go	ぞ zo	ど do		ぼ bo	ぽ po		

Writing Basics かくときの きほん

❑ What is a stroke?

A stroke begins when the pen (or any other writing device) comes in contact with the paper. The stroke ends when the pen separates from the paper.

❑ Why use brushes to write?

Traditionally, Japanese was written with brushes. This book – and almost any book that teaches Japanese writing – uses the brush-written style for the Japanese characters. The brush-written style best represents how the characters should be written.

❑ Different types of brush strokes

There are three types of strokes. For ease of understanding we have named them *fade out*, *dead stop* and *bounce fade*. Whether writing with a brush, pen, or pencil, make sure that you pay attention to the stroke type. This will ensure that your writing is neat and proper.

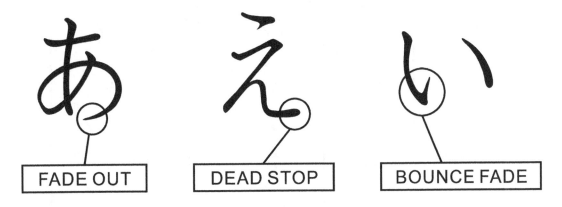

If your teacher is Japanese you might hear the Japanese names of the stroke types:

Fade out – harai (harau)
Dead stop – tome (tomeru)
Bounce fade – hane (haneru)

New Hiragana あたらしい ひらがな

The first five hiragana to learn are listed below. Notice the different stroke types. Be sure to learn the correct stroke order and stroke type.

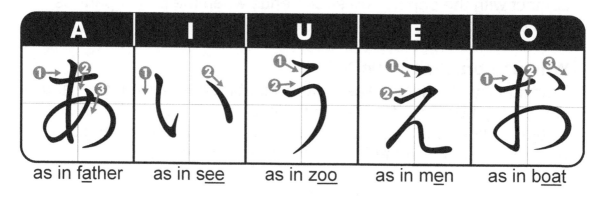

A	I	U	E	O
as in f<u>a</u>ther	as in s<u>ee</u>	as in z<u>oo</u>	as in m<u>e</u>n	as in b<u>oa</u>t

Various Styles スタイル

Write each symbol as neatly as you can in the writing practice section, then compare it to the different versions below.

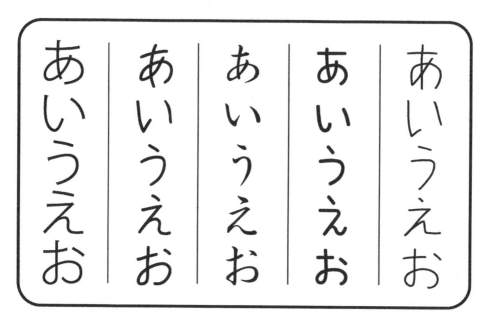

❑ The importance of the various styles

It is important to know what is allowed when writing. Remember that there are small differences between how the characters will look when writing with a brush and writing with a pen or pencil.

Writing Points かくポイント

❑ The difference between あ (a) and お (o)

Be careful not to mix up あ and お. The second stroke of あ is curved while the second stroke for お is straight until the loop.

more curved than お and not connected to the loop.

straighter than あ and connected to the loop.

❑ Writing left-to-right and top-to-bottom

Before World War II, most Japanese publications were written from top to bottom as shown in style 2. In modern Japan, the style used is based solely on design choice, and in some cases (such as writing an e-mail) only style 1 is possible. Many Japanese writing books for children will use style 2. *From Zero!* contains only style 1.

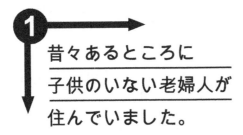

1
昔々あるところに
子供のいない老婦人が
住んでいました。

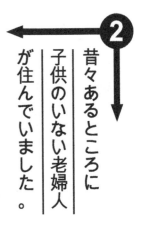

2
昔々あるところに
子供のいない老婦人
が住んでいました。

Writing Practice れんしゅう

Trace the light gray characters, then write each character six times.

a	あ	あ						
i	い	い						
u	う	う						
e	え	え						
o	お	お						

Word Practice ことばの れんしゅう

Fill in the appropriate hiragana in the blanks for each word.

1. ___ka___san (mother)
   o___a

2. _____ _____ (house)
   i___e

3. ___to___san (father)
   o___u

4. ___ka ___ (red)
   a___i

5. ___mo___to (younger sister)
   i___u

6. ka___ (to buy)
   u

7. ___sagi (rabbit)
   u

8. ___npitsu (pencil)
   e

9. ___ne___san (older sister)
   o___e

10. ___moshiro___ (interesting)
    o___i

11. ___su (chair)
    i

12. ___kiru (to wake up)
    o

Words You Can Write かける ことば

Write the following words using the hiragana that you just learned. This is a great way to increase your Japanese vocabulary.

a painting

え

good

いい

nephew

おい

love

あい

ray fish

えい

no

いいえ

many

おおい

to meet

あう

up

う	え										

to say

い	う										

house

い	え										

blue

あ	う										

Hiragana Matching ひらがな マッチング

Connect the dots between each hiragana and the correct ro–maji.

お ・   ・ a

う ・   ・ o

え ・   ・ u

い ・   ・ e

あ ・   ・ i

Everyday Hiragana Words にちじょうの ことば

あ kachan	い nu	う shi
baby	dog	cow

ka え ru

frog

お koru

to get mad

う chu う

space

Answer Key こたえ あわせ

No one likes to flip to the back of the book. Here are the answers.

❑Lesson 1: Word practice

1. お ka あ san
2. いえ
3. お to う san
4. あ ka い
5. い mo う to
6. ka う
7. う sagi
8. え npitsu
9. お ne え san
10. お moshiro い
11. い su
12. お kiru

❑Lesson 1: Hiragana matching

お	a
う	o
え	u
い	e
あ	i

Hiragana Practice Sheet れんしゅう

Lesson 2: Hiragana かきくけこ

New Hiragana あたらしい ひらがな

Correct stroke order will mean neater characters when writing quickly.

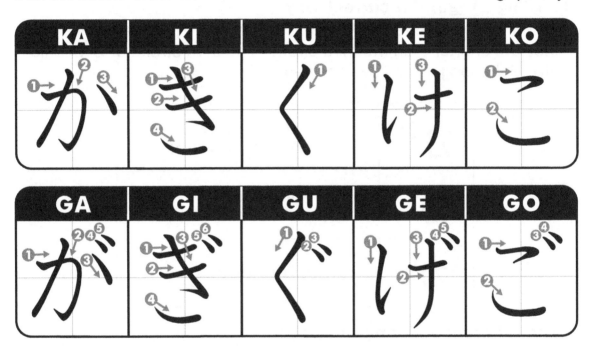

Various Styles スタイル

Write each symbol as neatly as you can, then compare it to the different versions below.

かきくけこ　かきくけこ　かきくけこ　かきくけこ　かきくけこ

がぎぐげご　がぎぐげご　がぎぐげご　がぎぐげご　がぎぐげご

Writing Points かくポイント

❏ The dakuten

The only difference between *ka ki ku ke ko* and *ga gi gu ge go* are the last two small strokes up in the right hand corner. Those strokes are called *dakuten*. You will see them often in future lessons.

❏ Writing が (ga) the correct way

When adding *dakuten* to か (ka) to make it が (ga), make sure that they are shorter than the third stroke. The third stroke of が should always be longer than the *dakuten*.

がﾟ	**INCORRECT** (dakuten are too long)
がﾞ	**INCORRECT** (dakuten are too short)
が	**CORRECT**

❏ The different versions of き (ki)

There are two versions of *ki*. It is your choice which version you use. You will see both in Japan depending on font or style choice.

き	This version has four strokes and is very common when writing. Many Japanese people write using this version.
き	This version has combined the third and fourth strokes into one stroke. It is very common in printed text such as books and magazines.

Writing Practice れんしゅう

First trace the gray characters, then write each character six times.

ka	か	か						
ki	き	き						
ku	く	く						
ke	け	け						
ko	こ	こ						

ga	が	が						
gi	ぎ	ぎ						
gu	ぐ	ぐ						
ge	げ	げ						
go	ご	ご						

Word Practice ことばの れんしゅう

Fill in the appropriate hiragana in the blanks for each word.

1. ___い ro   (yellow)
   ki

2. ___ ___   (to listen)
   ki ku

3. ___minari   (lightning)
   ka

4. ___う___n   (air force)
   ku   gu

5. ___ ___   (moss)
   ko ke

6. い___   (to go)
   ku

7. ___mushi   (caterpillar)
   ke

8. ___う___う   (airport)
   ku   ko

9. ___n い ro   (silver color)
   gi

10. ___n'ni___   (muscle)
    ki   ku

11. ___ ___   (afternoon)
    go   go

12. ___お ri   (ice)
    ko

Words You Can Write かける ことば

Write the following words using the hiragana that you just learned. This is a great way to increase your Japanese vocabulary.

tree

き

to write

か く

squid

い か

key

か	ぎ										

face

か	お										

shell

か	い										

red

あ	か										

afternoon, PM

ご	ご										

air

く	う	き							

foreign country

が	い	こ	く					

big

お	お	き	い					

airport

く	う	こ	う					

Hiragana Matching ひらがな マッチング
Connect the dots between each hiragana and the correct ro–maji.

き・   ・i

い・   ・go

く・   ・ka

か・   ・ki

え・   ・ku

ご・   ・ke

け・   ・e

Everyday Hiragana Words にちじょうの ことば

tsu き
the moon

けい ta い denwa
cell phone

かぎ
key

cho き n ba こ
safe, piggy
bank

かく
to write

su いか
watermelon

Answer Key こたえ あわせ

❏ Lesson 2: Word Practice

1. きい ro
3. か minari
5. こけ
7. け mushi
9. ぎ n い ro
11. ごご

2. きく
4. くうぐ n
6. いく
8. くうこう
10. き n'ni く
12. こお ri

❏ Lesson 2: Hiragana matching

き   i
い   go
く   ka
か   ki
え   ku
ご   ke
け   e

Hiragana Practice Sheet れんしゅう

Lesson 3: Hiragana さしすせそ

New Hiragana あたらしい ひらがな

Correct stroke order will mean neater characters when writing quickly.

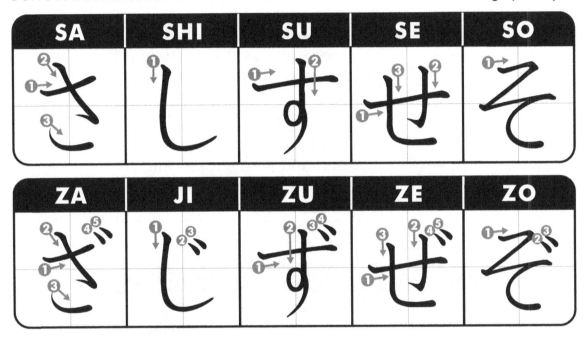

Various Styles スタイル

Write each symbol as neatly as you can, then compare it to the different versions below.

さしすせそ さしすせそ さしすせそ さしすせそ さしすせそ

ざじずぜぞ ざじずぜぞ ざじずぜぞ ざじずぜぞ ざじずぜぞ

Writing Points かくポイント

❏ The different versions of さ (sa) and そ (so)

You may have noticed in the *Various Styles* section of this lesson that there are two versions of *sa* and *so*. You can write whichever version you choose, so long as it is legible.

Different versions of さ (sa)	
さ	This version has three strokes and is very common when writing. Most Japanese people use this version when writing.
さ	This version has combined the second and third strokes into one stroke. It is very common in printed text.

Different versions of そ (so)	
そ	This version has two strokes and is common when writing. Many Japanese people write using this version.
そ	This version similar to version above except that the first and second stroke are touching.
そ	This version has only one stroke and is very common in printed text. It is also acceptable for writing.

Writing Practice れんしゅう

First trace the gray characters, then write each character six times.

sa	さ	さ						
shi	し	し						
su	す	す						
se	せ	せ						
so	そ	そ						

za	ざ	ざ						
ji	じ	じ						
zu	ず	ず						
ze	ぜ	ぜ						
zo	ぞ	ぞ						

Word Practice ことばの れんしゅう

Fill in the appropriate hiragana in the blanks for each word.

1. mura___き (purple)

sa

2. ___ ___ (to point)

sa   su

3. ___ro (white)

shi

4. ___tsugyo う (graduation)

so

5. ___ ___ (sushi)

su   shi

6. ___か n (time)

ji

7. ___ru (monkey)

sa

8. お___い___n (grandfather)

ji   sa

9. あ___ (sweat)

se

10. あ n___n (safety)

ze

11. ___う (elephant)

zo

12. げ n___い (currently, at present)

za

Words You Can Write かける ことば

Write the following words using the hiragana that you just learned.

deer

し	か								

sushi

す	し								

fire

か	じ								

cow

う	し									

numbers / amount

か	ず									

legs / feet

あ	し									

chair

い	す									

like

す	き									

slow / late

お	そ	い						

number

す	う	じ						

family

か	ぞ	く						

world

せ	か	い						

watermelon

す	い	か								

cool (temperature)

す	ず	し	い						

Hiragana Matching ひらがな マッチング

Connect the dots between each hiragana and the correct ro–maji.

す ·　　　· za

し ·　　　· su

え ·　　　· ku

こ ·　　　· shi

ざ ·　　　· i

あ ·　　　· e

く ·　　　· ko

い ·　　　· a

Everyday Hiragana Words にちじょうの ことば

ず bon
pants

し nbun
newspaper

tsu くえ
desk

さ mu い
cold

wa くせい
planet

すし
sushi

Answer Key こたえ あわせ

❏ Lesson 3: Word practice

1. mura さき
2. さす
3. し ro
4. そ tsugyo う
5. すし
6. じか n
7. さ ru
8. おじいさ n
9. あせ
10. あ n ぜ n
11. ぞう
12. げ n ざい

❏ Lesson 3: Hiragana matching

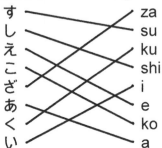

すし　　　　za
すし　　　　su
しえ　　　　ku
えこ　　　　shi
こざ　　　　i
ざあ　　　　e
あく　　　　ko
くい　　　　a

Hiragana Practice Sheet れんしゅう

Lesson 4: Hiragana たちつてと

New Hiragana あたらしい ひらがな

Correct stroke order will mean neater characters when writing quickly.

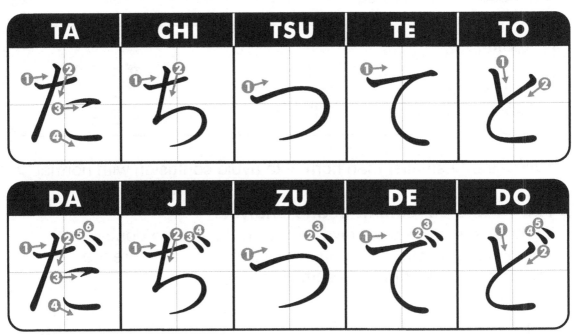

Various Styles スタイル

Write each symbol as neatly as you can, then compare it to the different versions below.

たちつてと　たちつてと　たちつてと　たちつてと　たちつてと

だぢづでど　だぢづでど　だぢづでど　だぢづでど　だぢづでど

Writing Points かくポイント

❏ **The double consonants**

The double consonants (*kk*, *pp*, *tt*, *cch*) are stressed with a slight pause before the consonant. To represent them in hiragana, a small つ is used.* The small つ is always placed in front of the hiragana that needs to be doubled.

> **Examples**
> school   ga<u>kk</u>ou   が<u>っこ</u>う
> magazine   za<u>ss</u>hi   ざ<u>っし</u>
> postage stamp   ki<u>tt</u>e   き<u>って</u>

* Write the つ smaller than normal to avoid confusion with normal つ.

❏ **The double consonant sound analysis**

If you look at the sound wave for a word that has a double consonant, you will see a pause or visible space before the consonant. Look at the two samples below:

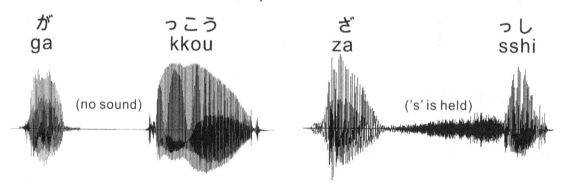

が　　　　　　　っこう　　　　　　　ざ　　　　　　　っし
ga　　　　　　　kkou　　　　　　　za　　　　　　　sshi
(no sound)　　　　　　　('s' is held)

❏ **Which version of *zu* and *ji* should be used?**

There are two versions of *zu* and *ji*. The first set is in Lesson 3. ず and じ are more commonly used. づ and ぢ are used in only a few words, such as は na ぢ (nosebleed) and つづく (to continue). If you're not sure about what version to use, try ず and じ and 90% of the time you will be correct.

❑ **The つ sound**

To say つ, start with the "TS" sound of "BOOTS" then add an
う sound.

Writing Practice れんしゅう

First trace the gray characters, then write each character six times.

ta	た	た					
chi	ち	ち					
tsu	つ	つ					
te	て	て					
to	と	と					

da	だ	だ					
ji	ぢ	ぢ					
zu	づ	づ					
de	で	で					
do	ど	ど					

Word Practice ことばの れんしゅう

Fill in the appropriate hiragana in the blanks for each word.

1. wa___し (me, I)
   ta

2. ___ ___ (free, no charge)
   ta   da

3. ___ ___ (to stand)
   ta   tsu

4. ___ ___ぜn (all of a sudden)
   to   tsu

5. ___ ___mu (to shrink)
   chi   ji

6. ___ ___ ___う (to help)
   te   tsu   da

7. い___い (it hurts, ouch)
   ta

8. お ___うさn (father)
   to

9. hana___ (nose bleed)
   ji

10. いき___mari (dead end)
    do

11. ___nwa (telephone)
    de

12. ___ ___く (to reach, arrive)
    to   do

Words You Can Write かける ことば

Write the following words using the hiragana that you just learned.

free

た	だ								

next

つ	ぎ								

map

ち	ず								

corner

か	ど										

map

ち	ず										

my father

ち	ち										

to stand

た	つ										

poison

ど	く										

magazine

ざ	っ	し								

postage stamp

き	っ	て								

hot

あ	づ	い								

far

と	お	い								

to deliver

と	ど	く									

continuation

つ	づ	き									

physical education

た	い	い	く							

Hiragana Matching ひらがな マッチング

Connect the dots between each hiragana and the correct ro–maji.

て ·　　　　· tsu

つ ·　　　　· da

さ ·　　　　· chi

ち ·　　　　· te

す ·　　　　· u

ぢ ·　　　　· ji

う ·　　　　· sa

だ ·　　　　· su

Everyday Hiragana Words にちじょうの ことば

で n し renji
microwave oven

hon だ na
bookshelf

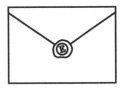

fu うとう
envelope

て
hand

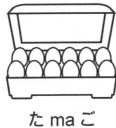

た ma ご
eggs

くつした
socks

Answer Key こたえ あわせ

❏ Lesson 4: Word practice

1. wa たし
2. ただ
3. たつ
4. とつぜ n
5. ちぢ mu
6. てつだう
7. いたい
8. おとうさ n
9. hana ぢ
10. いきど mari
11. で nwa
12. とどく

❏ Lesson 4: Hiragana matching

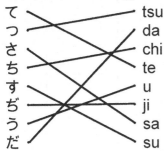

て　　　　tsu
っ　　　　da
さ　　　　chi
ち　　　　te
す　　　　u
ぢ　　　　ji
う　　　　sa
だ　　　　su

Hiragana Practice Sheet れんしゅう

Lesson 5: Hiragana なにぬねの

New Hiragana あたらしい ひらがな

Correct stroke order will mean neater characters when writing quickly.

NA	NI	NU	NE	NO
な	に	ぬ	ね	の

Various Styles スタイル

Write each symbol as neatly as you can, then compare it to the different versions below.

な に ぬ ね の	な に ぬ ね の	な に ぬ ね の	な に ぬ ね の	な に ぬ ね の

Writing Practice れんしゅう

First trace the gray characters, then write each character six times.

na	な	な					
ni	に	に					
nu	ぬ	ぬ					
ne	ね	ね					
no	の	の					

Word Practice ことばの れんしゅう

Fill in the appropriate hiragana in the blanks for each word.

1. ___つ (summer)
   na

2. ___hon (Japan)
   ni

3. ___こ (cat)
   ne

4. yo___か (middle of the night)
   na

5. ___mu (to drink)
   no

6. ___ru (to sleep, to go to bed)
   ne

7. ___ ___ (what?)
   na ni

8. ___いぐ rumi (stuffed animal)
   nu

9. ___がい (bitter tasting)
   ni

10. お___えさ n (older sister)
    ne

11. ___ぐ (to take off clothes)
    nu

12. ___ru (to ride)
    no

Words You Can Write かける ことば

Write the following words using the hiragana that you just learned.

what?

| な | に | | | | | | | | | | |

cat

| ね | こ | | | | | | | | | | |

seven (7)

| な | な | | | | | | | | | | |

west

| に | し | | | | | | | | | | |

summer

| な | つ | | | | | | | | | | |

fever

| ね | つ | | | | | | | | | | |

dog

| い | ぬ | | | | | | | | | | |

throat

| の | ど | | | | | | | | | | |

crab

かに

rainbow

にじ

meat

にく

inside

なか

brain

のう

you

あなた

diary

にっき

kitten

こねこ

lukewarm, tepid

ぬくい

Hiragana Matching ひらがな マッチング

Connect the dots between each hiragana and the correct ro–maji.

な ·	· no
の ·	· ni
か ·	· ta
す ·	· na
ぬ ·	· ka
ね ·	· nu
に ·	· ne
た ·	· su

Everyday Hiragana Words にちじょうの ことば

いぬ
dog

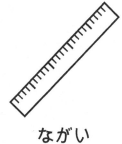

ながい
long

に wa と ri
chicken

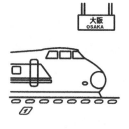

の ru

to ride

ぬ ru

to paint

ねこ

cat

Answer Key こたえ あわせ

❏ Lesson 5: Word practice

1. なつ
2. に hon
3. ねこ
4. yo なか
5. の mu
6. ね ru
7. なに
8. ぬいぐ rumi
9. にがい
10. おねえさ n
11. ぬぐ
12. の ru

❏ Lesson 5: Hiragana matching

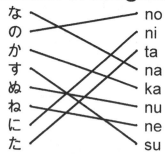

な   no
の   ni
か   ta
す   na
ぬ   ka
ね   nu
に   ne
た   su

Lesson 6: Hiragana はひふへほ

New Hiragana あたらしい ひらがな

Correct stroke order will mean neater characters when writing quickly.

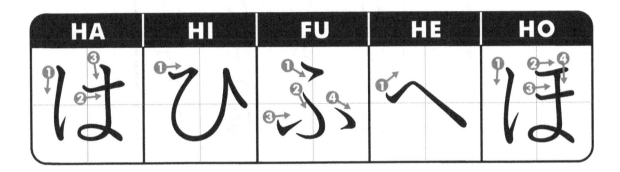

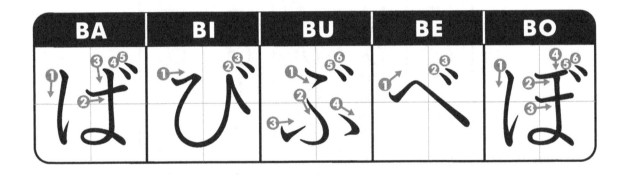

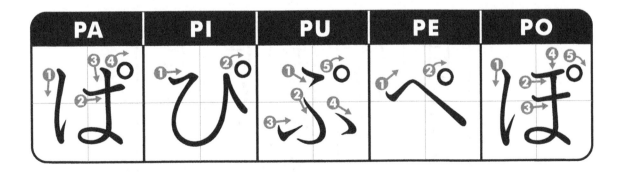

Various Styles スタイル

Write each symbol as neatly as you can, then compare it to the different versions below.

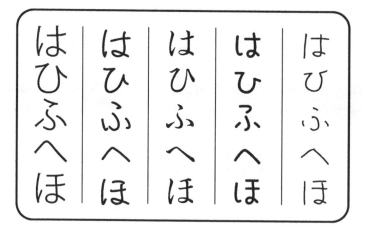

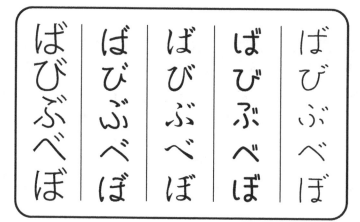

Writing Points かくポイント

❏ What is that circle?

The *pa pi pu pe po* hiragana are made by adding a circle in the area where *dakuten* normally would go. The circle should be written clockwise and is always the last stroke. Most Japanese people refer to this as simply *maru*, which means "circle." The official name for it is *handakuten.*

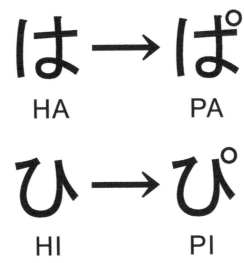

は → ぱ
HA   PA

ひ → ぴ
HI   PI

❏ Why isn't ふ written as *HU*?

Japanese From Zero! represents ふ as *FU* instead of *HU* in ro–maji. Japanese people will sometimes represent ふ as *HU* in ro–maji, however, the pronunciation of ふ is closer to *FU*. The F sound in ふ should be voiced softer than the F sound in an English word.

❏ The easy way to write ふ (fu)

ふ tends to be difficult to write, but there is an easy way: connect the first and second stroke into what looks like a number "3."

ふ   ふ ふ ふ

The 3 Version   Actual Font Versions

Writing Practice れんしゅう

First trace the gray characters, then write each character six times.

ha	は	は						
hi	ひ	ひ						
fu	ふ	ふ						
he	へ	へ						
ho	ほ	ほ						

ba	ば	ば						
bi	び	び						
bu	ぶ	ぶ						
be	べ	べ						
bo	ぼ	ぼ						

pa	ぱ	ぱ						
pi	ぴ	ぴ						
pu	ぷ	ぷ						
pe	ぺ	ぺ						
po	ぽ	ぽ						

Special Usage とくべつな つかいかた

❏ The topic marker は (wa)

A topic marker in Japanese identifies the subject of a sentence.
The topic marker "wa" is written using the は (ha) character and can never be written using the わ (wa) character. In all other situations, は (ha) is always read as "ha."

> **Example Sentences**
> 1. あなたは (wa) だ re ですか。
>   Who are you?
>
> 2. Banana は (wa) きい ro です。
>   Bananas are yellow.

❏ The direction marker へ (e)

The direction marker "e" is written using the へ (he) character and can never be written using the え (e) character. In all other situations, へ (he) is always read as "he."

Example Sentences

1. がっこうへ (e) いき ma す。
   I am going towards (to) school.

2. とう kyo うへ (e) いき ma す。
   I am going towards (to) Tokyo.

Word Practice ことばの れんしゅう

Fill in the appropriate hiragana in the blanks for each word.

1. ___ru   (spring)
   <u>ha</u>

2. ___ru ご___n   (lunch)
   <u>hi</u>   <u>ha</u>

3. ___yu   (winter)
   <u>fu</u>

4. ___い wa   (peace)
   <u>he</u>

5. え___n   (picture book)
   <u>ho</u>

6. が n___ru   (to do your best)
   <u>ba</u>

7. ___な___   (fireworks)
   <u>ha</u>   <u>bi</u>

8. か mi___く ro   (paper bag)
   <u>bu</u>

9. ___と me___re   (love at first sight)
   <u>hi</u>   <u>bo</u>

10. く ra___ru   (to compare)
    <u>be</u>

11. ___ ___な   (electric spark)
    <u>hi</u> <u>ba</u>

12. え n___つ   (pencil)
    <u>pi</u>

Words You Can Write かける ことば

Write the following words using the hiragana that you just learned.

chopsticks, bridge

は	し									

star (in sky)

ほ	し									

lid, top

ふ	た									

belly button

へ	そ									

pigeon, dove

は	と									

pig

ぶ	た									

person

ひ	と									

to dry

ほ	す									

tail

| し | っ | ぽ | | | | | | | | | |

tofu (soy bean)

| と | う | ふ | | | | | | | | | |

leaf

| は | っ | ぱ | | | | | | | | | |

cheeks

| ほ | っ | ぺ | | | | | | | | | |

hat

| ぼ | う | し | | | | | | | | | |

ticket

| き | っ | ぷ | | | | | | | | | |

fireworks

| は | な | び | | | | | | | | | |

tall person, bean pole

| の | っ | ぽ | | | | | | | | | |

first love

| は | つ | こ | い | | | | | | | | |

Hiragana Matching ひらがな マッチング

Connect the dots between each hiragana and the correct ro–maji.

ふ ・   ・ pi

ぺ ・   ・ pe

ぜ ・   ・ bo

ぼ ・   ・ gi

は ・   ・ fu

た ・   ・ ze

ぴ ・   ・ ta

ぎ ・   ・ ha

Everyday Hiragana Words にちじょうの ことば

ひ sho
secretary

ふく ro う
owl

おばけ
monster

ほうたい
bandage

はし ru
to run

てっぽう
pistol, gun

Answer Key こたえ あわせ

☐ Lesson 6: Word Practice

1. は ru
2. ひ ru ごは n
3. ふ yu
4. へい wa
5. えほ n
6. が n ば ru
7. はなび
8. か mi ぶく ro
9. ひと me ぼ re
10. く ra べ ru
11. ひばな
12. え n ぴつ

☐ Lesson 6: Hiragana matching

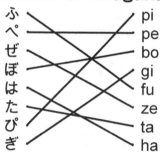

ふ — pi
ぺ — pe
ぜ — bo
ぼ — gi
は — fu
た — ze
ぴ — ta
ぎ — ha

Lesson 7: Hiragana まみむめも

New Hiragana あたらしい ひらがな

Correct stroke order will mean neater characters when writing quickly.

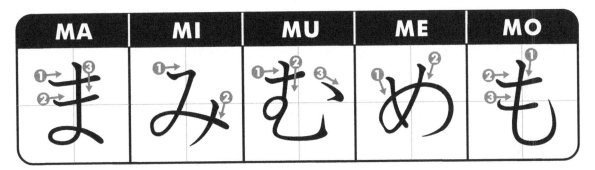

MA	MI	MU	ME	MO

Various Styles スタイル

Write each symbol as neatly as you can, then compare it to the different versions below.

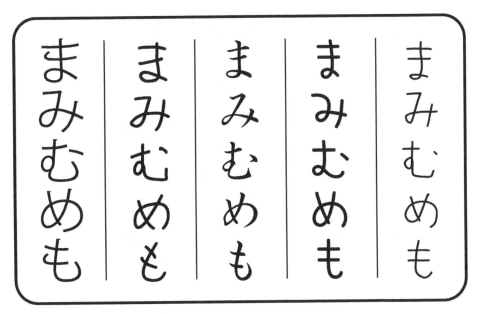

Writing Practice れんしゅう

First trace the gray characters, then write each character six times.

ma	ま	ま					
mi	み	み					
mu	む	む					
me	め	め					
mo	も	も					

Word Practice ことばの れんしゅう

Fill in the appropriate hiragana in the blanks for each word.

1. ___ri (forest)
   mo

2. ___ ___じ (maple leaf)
   mo mi

3. ___ri (impossible)
   mu

4. ___だつ (to stand out)
   me

5. ___ru (to see, to watch)
   mi

6. ___がね (eye glasses)
   me

7. たべ___の (food)
   mo

8. ___ ___ru (to protect)
   ma mo

9. の___ ___の (a drink)
     mi mo

10. ___しあつい (humid)
    mu

11.___ほう (magic)
  ma

12. ___ ___ず (earthworm)
    mi mi

Words You Can Write かける ことば

Write the following words using the hiragana that you just learned.

window

まど									

peach

もも									

miso, bean paste

みそ									

insect

むし									

hair, god, paper

かみ									

no good

だめ									

store

みせ									

cicada, locust

せみ

head

あたま

nick name

あだな

serious

まじめ

sashimi

さしみ

son

むすこ

daughter

むすめ

short

みじかい

ruler

ものさし

Hiragana Matching ひらがな マッチング

Connect the dots between each hiragana and the correct ro–maji.

に・   ・mu

む・   ・mi

も・   ・nu

ぬ・   ・ni

み・   ・o

ま・   ・mo

お・   ・me

め・   ・ma

Everyday Hiragana Words にちじょうの ことば

yoむ
to read

のみもの
a drink

しつもn
question

なみだ

tears

うま

horse

あめ

candy

Answer Key こたえ あわせ

❑**Lesson 7: Word practice**

1. も ri	2. もみじ
3. む ri	4. めだつ
5. みる	6. めがね
7. たべもの	8. まも ru
9. のみもの	10. むしあつい
11. まほう	12. みみず

❑**Lesson 7: Hiragana matching**

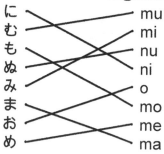

に	mu
む	mi
も	nu
ぬ	ni
み	o
ま	mo
お	me
め	ma

Lesson 8: Hiragana やゆよわをん

New Hiragana あたらしい ひらがな

Correct stroke order will mean neater characters when writing quickly.

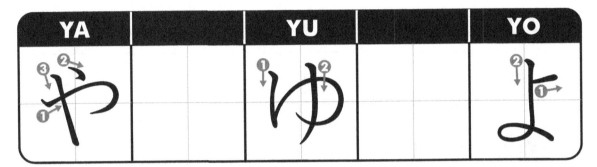

Various Styles スタイル

Write each symbol as neatly as you can, then compare it to the different versions below.

Writing Practice れんしゅう

First trace the gray characters, then write each character six times.

ya	や	や						
yu	ゆ	ゆ						
yo	よ	よ						
wa	わ	わ						
wo	を	を						
n	ん	ん						

Word Practice ことばの れんしゅう

Fill in the appropriate hiragana in the blanks for each word.

1. ___ra う   (to laugh)
   wa

2. だいこ___   (radish)
   n

3. みず___のむ   (to drink water)
   wo

4. ___ru い   (bad)
   wa

5. ___たし   (me, I)
   wa

6. ほ___ ___かう   (buy a book)
   n   wo

7. こ___ ___ (tonight, this evening)
     <u>n</u> <u>ya</u>

8. ___す reru (to forget)
  <u>wa</u>

9. えいが ___み ru (to watch a movie)
     <u>wo</u>

10. き___ぞく (metal)
    <u>n</u>

11. か___た___ (easy)
   <u>n</u>   <u>n</u>

12. すし___たべ ru (to eat sushi)
     <u>wo</u>

Special Usage とくべつな つかいかた

❑ **The particle を (wo)**
The hiragana を is only used as a particle (object marker). It is never used for any other purpose. Even though "wo" is normally pronounced "o", お can never replace を as a particle.

Example Sentences
1. てがみを (wo) かきます。   I will write a letter.
2. えんぴつを (wo) ください。 Give me a pencil please.

Words You Can Write かける ことば

Write the following words using the hiragana that you just learned.

alligator

わ	に								

roof

や	ね								

finger

ゆ	び								

garden

に	わ									

last night

ゆ	う	べ								

ring

ゆ	び	わ								

seaweed

わ	か	め								

tonight

こ	ん	や								

rumor

う	わ	さ								

(rice) paddy

た	ん	ぼ								

easy

か	ん	た	ん						

human being

に	ん	げ	ん						

Hiragana Matching ひらがな マッチング

Connect the dots between each hiragana and the correct ro–maji.

は・	・yu
よ・	・to
ゆ・	・n
わ・	・wo (o)
と・	・ha
や・	・wa
を・	・yo
ん・	・ya

Everyday Hiragana Words にちじょうの ことば

たいよう
the sun

うわぎ
jacket

ゆかた
light kimono

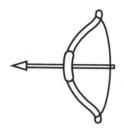

ゆみや

bow and arrow

かわかす

to dry

じてん sha

bicycle

Answer Key こたえ あわせ

❏ Lesson 8: Word practice

1. わ ra う
2. だいこん
3. みずを のむ
4. わ ru い
5. わたし
6. ほんを かう
7. こんや
8. わす reru
9. えいがを み ru
10. きんぞく
11. かんたん
12. すしを たべ ru

❏ Lesson 8: Hiragana matching

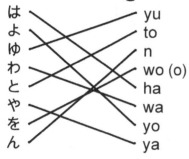

は   yu
よ   to
ゆ   n
わ   wo (o)
と   ha
や   wa
を   yo
ん   ya

Lesson 9: Hiragana らりるれろ

New Hiragana あたらしい ひらがな

Correct stroke order will mean neater characters when writing quickly.

RA	RI	RU	RE	
ら	り	る	れ	ろ

Various Styles スタイル

Write each symbol as neatly as you can, then compare it to the different versions below.

ら	ら	ら	ら	ら
り	り	り	り	り
る	る	る	る	る
れ	れ	れ	れ	れ
ろ	ろ	ろ	ろ	ろ

Writing Practice れんしゅう

First trace the gray characters, then write each character six times.

ra	ら	ら						
ri	り	り						
ru	る	る						
re	れ	れ						
ro	ろ	ろ						

Word Practice ことばの れんしゅう

Fill in the appropriate hiragana in the blanks for each word.

1. あた___しい (new)
ra

2. し___ (to know)
ru

3. ___んあい (true love)
re

4. ___んご (apple)
ri

5. みせ___ (to show)
ru

6. ___ん shu う (practice)
re

7. べん___ (convenient)
ri

8. う___おい (moisture)
ru

9. かく___んぼ (hide and seek)
re

10. どう___ (road)
ro

11. ___うか (hallway)
ro

12. まわ___みち (detour)
ri

Words You Can Write かける ことば

Write the following words using the hiragana that you just learned.

science

り	か										

night

よ	る										

impossible

む	り										

example

れ	い										

circle

ま	る										

monkey

さ	る										

ice

こ	お	り									

duck

あ	ひ	る									

camel

ら	く	だ								

frog, to return

か	え	る								

apple

り	ん	ご								

convenient

べ	ん	り								

left

ひ	だ	り								

management

か	ん	り								

yellow

き	い	ろ								

light blue

み	ず	い	ろ							

candle

ろ	う	そ	く							

Hiragana Matching ひらがな マッチング

Connect the dots between each hiragana and the correct ro–maji.

る ・	・ ru
し ・	・ shi
り ・	・ re
ろ ・	・ i
ぬ ・	・ ro
れ ・	・ ra
い ・	・ nu
ら ・	・ ri

Everyday Hiragana Words にちじょうの ことば

ねる
to sleep, go to bed

いくら
salted salmon eggs

くすり
medicine

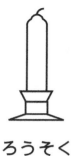

ろうそく
candle

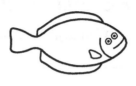

かれい
flounder

かみなり
thunder, lightning

Answer Key こたえ あわせ

❏ Lesson 9: Word practice

1. あたらしい
2. しる
3. れんあい
4. りんご
5. みせる
6. れん shu う
7. べんり
8. うるおい
9. かくれんぼ
10. どうろ
11. ろうか
12. まわりみち

❏ Lesson 9: Hiragana matching

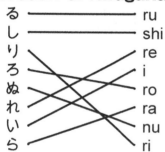

る ─────── ru
し ─────── shi
り　　　　　　　re
ろ　　　　　　　i
ぬ　　　　　　　ro
れ　　　　　　　ra
い　　　　　　　nu
ら　　　　　　　ri

Lesson 10: Compound Hiragana

New Hiragana あたらしい ひらがな

The final hiragana are easy! There are only 33 official hiragana left to learn - but don't let that number scare you. They are all made up of the hiragana that you already know. Just by looking at them you should already have an idea of the sound that they represent.

> **Examples**
>
> き (ki)   +   や (ya)   =   きゃ (kya)
>
> し (shi)   +   ゆ (yu)   =   しゅ (shu)
>
> ち (chi)   +   よ (yo)   =   ちょ (cho)

As you can see you add a small version of や、ゆ or よ to items in the い form of the hiragana.

Writing Points かくポイント

❑ **The correct way to write compound hiragana**
   When writing compound hiragana, make sure that the second character is visibly smaller than the first character.

ro–maji	correct	incorrect
mya	みゃ	みや
ryo	りょ	りよ
chu	ちゅ	ちゆ
kya	きゃ	きや
pya	ぴゃ	ぴや

❏ Compound Hiragana

The following are the compound hiragana. They are created using the hiragana you already know so you should have no problem learning these.

きゃ kya	きゅ kyu	きょ kyo		ひゃ hya	ひゅ hyu	ひょ hyo
ぎゃ gya	ぎゅ gyu	ぎょ gyo		びゃ bya	びゅ byu	びょ byo
しゃ sha	しゅ shu	しょ sho		ぴゃ pya	ぴゅ pyu	ぴょ pyo
じゃ ja	じゅ ju	じょ jo		みゃ mya	みゅ myu	みょ myo
ちゃ cha	ちゅ chu	ちょ cho		りゃ rya	りゅ ryu	りょ ryo
にゃ nya	にゅ nyu	にょ nyo				

Writing Practice れんしゅう

First trace the gray characters, then write each character six times.

KYA きゃ

KYU きゅ

KYO きょ

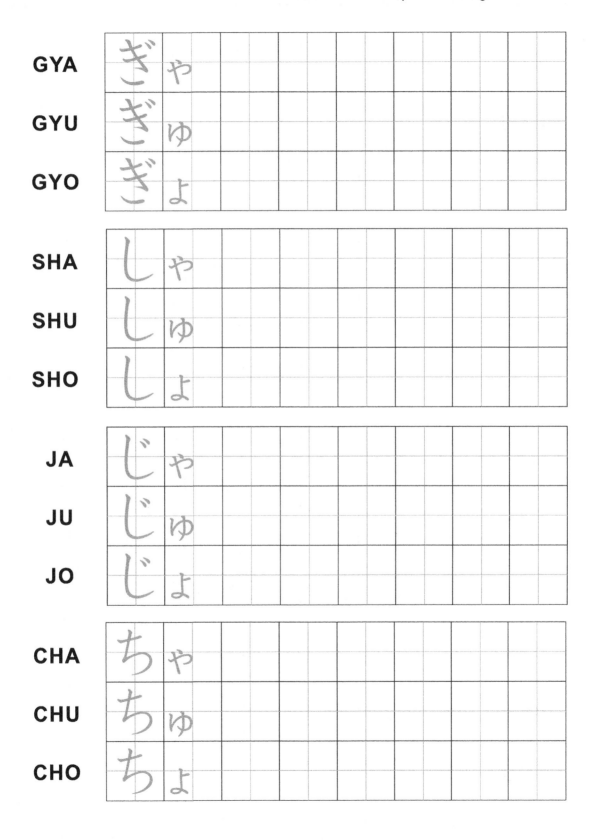

GYA	ぎゃ							
GYU	ぎゅ							
GYO	ぎょ							

SHA	しゃ							
SHU	しゅ							
SHO	しょ							

JA	じゃ							
JU	じゅ							
JO	じょ							

CHA	ちゃ							
CHU	ちゅ							
CHO	ちょ							

NYA	にゃ							
NYU	にゅ							
NYO	にょ							

HYA	ひゃ							
HYU	ひゅ							
HYO	ひょ							

BYA	びゃ							
BYU	びゅ							
BYO	びょ							

PYA	ぴゃ							
PYU	ぴゅ							
PYO	ぴょ							

MYA	みゃ							
MYU	みゅ							
MYO	みょ							

RYA	りゃ							
RYU	りゅ							
RYO	りょ							

Word Practice ことばの れんしゅう

Fill in the appropriate hiragana in the blanks for each word.

1. とう___く (arrival)
   cha

2. さん___く (three hundred)
   bya

3. と___かん (library)
   sho

4. ___う___う (cow's milk)
   gyu   nyu

5. さん___く (mountain range)
   mya

6. ___うばい (business, commerce)
   sho

7. ___うたん (carpet)
   ju

8. でん___う (sales slip, voucher)
   pyo

9. ___うだい (siblings)
    kyo

10. ___う___う (dinosaur)
     kyo   ryu

11. ___うがく (study abroad)
    ryu

12. ___うどん (beef bowl)
    gyu

Words You Can Write かける ことば

Write the following words using the compound hiragana that you just learned.

butterfly

ちょう										

nine (9)

きゅう										

pulse

みゃく										

dragon

りゅう										

reverse

ぎゃく										

song

きょく										

company

かいしゃ

sickness, sick

びょうき

veterinarian

じゅうい

Kyoto

きょうと

repair

しゅうり

travel

りょこう

train

でんしゃ

goldfish

きんぎょ

bowl

ちゃわん

Hiragana Matching ひらがな マッチング

Connect the dots between each hiragana and the correct ro–maji.

ぎゃ ·	· nyu
みょ ·	· shu
しゅ ·	· rya
ぴょ ·	· ja
りゃ ·	· myo
ちょ ·	· pyo
じゃ ·	· cho
にゅ ·	· gya

Everyday Hiragana Words にちじょうの ことば

ちきゅうぎ
globe

しゅう
state

おちゃ
tea

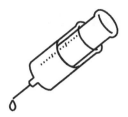

べんきょう
study

ちゅうしゃ
shot

しゅうり
repair

Answer Key こたえ あわせ

❏ Lesson 10: Word practice

1. とうちゃく
2. さんびゃく
3. としょかん
4. ぎゅうにゅう
5. さんみゃく
6. しょうばい
7. じゅうたん
8. でんぴょう
9. きょうだい
10. きょうりゅう
11. りゅうがく
12. ぎゅうどん

❏ Lesson 10: Hiragana matching

ぎゃ   nyu
みょ   shu
しゅ   rya
ぴょ   ja
りゃ   myo
ちょ   pyo
じゃ   cho
にゅ   gya

Hiragana Practice Sheet れんしゅう

Lesson 11: The Next Step

Congratulations on learning hiragana!
Here are some tips to help you reinforce what you have learned:

Let's put hiragana in our daily lives!
Write words on "post it" notes and then stick them on items. You can write しお and こしょう on your salt and pepper shakers using a permanent marker. This reinforces your skills even when you aren't thinking about it.

Read manga!
Some manga (Japanese comics) and children books have small hiragana next to the kanji. This is called "furigana". Look for furigana when purchasing manga. It's like Japanese on training wheels!

Keep on learning!
Your next step is to learn katakana! You have come this far, so keep up the momentum. We are sure you will also enjoy learning katakana in "Katakana From Zero!".

Hiragana Cards

The next few pages can be cut out to make flash cards. Or you can just flip back and forth to see if you know the hiragana character.

あ	か	が
い	き	ぎ
う	く	ぐ
え	け	げ
お	こ	ご

ga	ka	a
gi	ki	i
gu	ku	u
ge	ke	e
go	ko	o

さ	ざ	た
し	じ	ち
す	ず	つ
せ	ぜ	て
そ	ぞ	と

ta	za	sa
chi	ji	shi
tsu	zu	su
te	ze	se
to	zo	so

だ	な	は
ぢ	に	ひ
づ	ぬ	ふ
で	ね	へ
ど	の	ほ

ha	na	da
hi	ni	ji
fu	nu	zu
he	ne	de
ho	no	do

ば	ぱ	ま
び	ぴ	み
ぶ	ぷ	む
べ	ぺ	め
ぼ	ぽ	も

ma	pa	ba
mi	pi	bi
mu	pu	bu
me	pe	be
mo	po	bo

や	る	ん
ゆ	れ	きゃ
よ	ろ	きゅ
ら	わ	きょ
り	を	ぎゃ

n	ru	ya
kya	re	yu
kyu	ro	yo
kyo	wa	ra
gya	wo	ri

ぎゅ	じゃ	ちょ
ぎょ	じゅ	にゃ
しゃ	じょ	にゅ
しゅ	ちゃ	にょ
しょ	ちゅ	ひゃ

cho	ja	gyu
nya	ju	gyo
nyu	jo	sha
nyo	cha	shu
hya	chu	sho

ひゅ	ぴゃ	みょ
ひょ	ぴゅ	りゃ
びゃ	ぴょ	りゅ
びゅ	みゃ	りょ
びょ	みゅ	

myo	pya	hyu
rya	pyu	hyo
ryu	pyo	bya
ryo	mya	byu
	myu	byo

Other From Zero! Books

Made in the USA
Middletown, DE
22 August 2023

37144360R00060